FACES OF
THE FRONTIER

FACES OF
THE FRONTIER

Written and illustrated by
Lorence F. Bjorklund

DODD, MEAD & COMPANY · NEW YORK

TO MY GIRLS
my wife Kay, my daughter Karna,
and my granddaughter, Kim Elizabeth

PREFACE

THERE is a custom prevailing in which one who writes a book precedes its contents with a prelude stating more or less why he undertook such a project. My reasons run something like this:

For many years I have been making drawings to illustrate other people's books, hoping to depict what they had in mind and to make more graphic that part which is ordinarily left between the lines. Rarely does an author go into exacting detail about the convolutions in the ears of his heroes, nor does he count the spokes in the hind wheel of a buckboard. But for an illustrator with a realistic bent, these things are routine matters. Some subjects are impractical to write about. For instance, a paragraph of clear instructions on how to tie the knot in a shoelace would be a most complicated literary feat, whereas a small sketch with a directional arrow here and there could make everything clear and understandable.

The West of the nineteenth century was bounded by a moving line called the frontier, which encompassed more than a vast expanse of geography, for it was made by people and was moved westward by people. It seemed to me that it would be interesting for a change to move up a little closer to those people and see the features usually obscured in the shadow of their wide-brimmed hats. So that close portraiture of these frontiersmen should not be empty magnification, some words were in order.

Since a pencil can be persuaded to write as well as draw, I sharpened a 2B Staedtler at both ends and set back the clock to the time of our grandfathers and somewhat beyond. The frontier had certainly waned when I was a boy, but there was enough of it remaining all over the West so that if you leaned on anything some of it would rub off on you. I didn't bother to dust any of it off so my hope is that a little sifted into this book to help dispel the odd notion that the whole thing was a myth.

LFB

CONTENTS

FACES OF
THE FRONTIER

THE INDIAN

At THE dawn of the nineteenth century, the red man was already there on the boundless ocean of grass, long before the vast spaces became a theater of dramatic events called America's frontier. Here, for hundreds of decades, his people had followed the buffalo unmolested, for on these shaggy animals depended his supply of food, clothing, and shelter. But at that dawning, the world of the red man began to change.

It started as a trickle of white men who explored the plains and navigated the rivers. After them came the trappers, men much like the Indian himself, in temperament and inclination, and following them came the missionaries. For these the Indian had some curiosity but no particular hostility, and there was no warning of the oncoming flood.

The wagons began to roll across the prairies and many more white men came to trespass the buffalo range. On the rimrocks the Indians sat their ponies, watching in wonder as the white-topped wagons grew ever more numerous and milled deep ruts in the turf. Slowly the old men of the tribes came to know that these people of the hairy faces and hard-soled moccasins were invaders. The Indians sharpened their tomahawks, put on the paint and war-bonnet, and braided feathers into the tails of their ponies. They filled their quivers with war arrows and rode down from the rimrocks. Some of the intruders were killed, but still more wagons came and the Indian, now fully aroused to the portent of it all, fought harder.

The soldiers came and built strong war-lodges and their leaders were sent to smoke with the chiefs, to shake hands over buried tomahawks, and sign solemn peace pacts. The white man broke the treaties, so the hatchets were dug up and scalplocks of blond hair fluttered from the warshields.

Then the white man, guarded by the soldiers, joined long pieces of steel and laid them in endless pairs over the plains to make a trail for his swift iron horse. He killed the buffalo to feed the tracklayers and to make carriage robes. He strung a talking wire that could send messages farther and faster than any smoke signal from the highest butte. The words that rode the wire told the soldiers the whereabouts of the Indian every time he moved and they pursued him unceasingly.

By the time night had fallen on the nineteenth century, the look of eagles had passed from the eyes of the Indian and the once numberless buffalo were reduced to a pile of bones.

IT SEEMS strange somehow to find a man attired in a tricorn hat and regimental tunic of the Continental Army far up on the steep slopes of a pass in the Rocky Mountains. But it is no anachronism, for the date was September 19, 1805, and the soldier was one of the party of men who shared the great adventure of the Captains, Lewis and Clark, as they explored the upper portion of the Louisiana Purchase. By commission of President Thomas Jefferson, the primary purpose of the expedition was to seek out prospects for fur trading in the newly acquired territory and the goal was to reach the Columbia River, whose mouth had been discovered in 1792 by Captain Robert Gray, a Boston skipper in the fur trade.

The explorers were guided by a Shoshone Indian girl, Sacajawea, who had been captured by the Minatarees and taken far from her home in the western mountains. Sacajawea was aptly named, for her name meant "Bird Woman" and with the instincts of a homing pigeon she led the trail blazers toward the Columbia.

On that day in September, with a blizzard hissing around them, the Captains were beset with doubts as they followed the girl over a dangerous and terrifying trail along a ridge. The diary of Meriwether Lewis, in the entry for that day, reads in part—"When the ridge terminated and we to our inexpresable joy discovered a large tract of Prairie country lying to the S.W. and widening as it appeared to extend to the W. Through that plain the Indian informed us that the Columbia river (in which we were in surch) run. This plain appeared to be about sixty miles distant, but our guide assured us that we should reach its border tomorrow."

THE
TRAIL BLAZER

THE VAQUERO

FROM across the Rio Grande, from Baja and Alta California, came the forerunner of the cowboy. While minutemen of New England were having their disagreement with George III, the vaquero was roping cattle on the Pacific side of the continent some three-quarters of a century before the stockman brought his herds to the plains.

He did the same work as the cowboy, but differently, and his accoutrements were dissimilar but accomplished the same end. To fend off the cacti, he wore *armitas* instead of chaps—thigh-wide leather strips that hung from his belt and extended to below the knees, where they were fastened by a strap. These were overlapped by leather leggings (*botas*) and instead of the familiar high-heeled boots, he wore soft shoes with low heels and upturned toes. Their counters were supplemented with heavy pieces of hide to hold up the big-roweled spurs.

His greatest skill was exhibited in the use of *la reata* (from whence comes our word, lariat). The *reata larga* was from seventy to one hundred feet long and was swung with a very large loop. A vaquero could use the artfully braided rawhide at its full length. In fact, the vaqueros of California would go on a grizzly bear chase armed only with the long lariats. Three horsemen would come across the big bear and, dashing up toward it, one roper would put his loop on from the left, another from the right, and the third hooked a hind leg and stretched the critter out flat!

The vaquero was a superb horseman and he sat with an easy grace in his big-horned rawhide saddle, from whence he could watch a hundred miles pass under his horse's hooves in one day without feeling the worse for it.

THE TRADING SKIPPER

IN SPITE of Spanish laws prohibiting foreign trade with the residents of early California, the Yankee barks and brigs did a booming business for some thirty years.

The craggy-faced skipper of a Boston brig would spend a year or two cruising up and down the long Pacific coast line, trading his goods for hides and tallow and selling the 'tween-decks cargo to anyone brave enough to be rowed through the swells to the anchored vessel.

The skipper carried necessities such as furniture, gunpowder, bolts of cloth, tools, pots, and needles as regular stock-in-trade, but prominently exhibited were items that had been picked up at some port in the Orient. Displays of jewelry and jade, pieces fashioned from rare woods or from ivory, Oriental rugs, and the highly desired embroidered shawls from China turned demure señoritas into wheedling harpies.

The skipper's supercargo rubbed his palms together happily when a goateed ranchero was cornered by several earnestly gesturing women from his hacienda. The ranchero probably had to run a *matanza* (slaughter) the next day to garner enough bales of hides to defray the cost of the finery. Because the hides were "green," the skipper had to be a tanner as well as trader and navigator, for it would be months before the ship would be back home. He would select a section of arid beach, perhaps near San Diego, and there put the crew to work to scrape the soaked hides clean of flesh. They were then thoroughly salted and racked up to dry. When the sun had done its work, the hides were folded, pressed, and hauled out to the ship, hoisted aboard and stowed below. When the brig's hold was stuffed to the carlings, the skipper gave the order to weigh anchor, h'ist the sails, and it was "Ho, for the Horn!" and then north to Boston.

THE
MOUNTAIN MAN

In THE years between 1820 and 1840 a hardy and reckless group of men roamed the mountain wilderness, making their living as fur trappers.

Their colorfully beaded and quilled clothing of skin and fur was crafted by the skillful needlework of their Indian wives. These costumes were best admired upwind, at long range, for once donned, the smoked buckskins were worn until they decayed.

To the bearded mountain men goes the credit for finding the passes and establishing pathways for the pioneers who followed in the long wagon trains. Armed with knife, tomahawk, and Hawken rifle, ever searching for new trapping grounds, these men explored canyons and river courses never before seen by anyone but the Indians.

Each summer the trappers would meet at a "rendezvous," previously agreed upon, to sell or trade their pelts to the big fur companies for trade goods or gold. As many as six hundred mountain men gathered at these fairs, where sometimes a man would barter the proceeds of a year's work for a few casks of Cincinnati whiskey, which with the help of his friends would be consumed on the spot.

With the relentless pursuit of the beaver and other animals whose skins were of value, the trapping grounds were so depleted by 1835 that the mountain man's way of life soon faded into history.

THE MISSIONARY

THOUGH most missionaries of the early West made little progress in converting any great number of either Indians or pioneers to Christianity, they made a major contribution to American history for which they are given little credit. Their letters and articles sent back to religious periodicals were filled with glowing prose praising their adopted Eden-like Oregon country and disease-free valleys of California. These writings were the propaganda which actually inspired the great westward migrations.

Long before the wagon tires of the pioneers crushed the buffalo grass, the missionaries were crossing the mountains and, finding there the paradise of the mountain men, they sought to expel sin from the few who lived in the beautiful land. In this endeavor their reports bespoke mediocre success, but the agricultural possibilities they wrote about were truly fabulous and the market prices for great quantities of produce and livestock were beyond belief. The letters that came back east passed from hand to hand, were printed and reprinted in newspapers, and a national itch for this Western Utopia resulted from the publicity.

Then the covered wagons began to roll, thousands of them, carrying the starry-eyed emigrants, and when they finally reached the promised land—either the Willamette or Sacramento valleys—there were the missions already established as the nucleus of communities and cities. And the missionaries looked at the westward rolling surge and then to one another and said, "God works in wondrous ways his wonders to perform."

THE FERRYBOAT WOMAN

"WELL, now I been runnin' this ferry by myself for quite a while and keepin' it in pretty fair shape too, considerin' everything.

"My husband built the scow and the ramps some ten years back an' we done pretty well on tolls as there's a sort of natural road leads down to here, an' the freight an' supplies for the Army comes over the hump by this trail reg'lar.

"My man run it for a couple years, but he got restless and joined up with some Rocky mountain trappers that come by. I used to get lonesome, but I got over it an' I keep busy at somethin'—well, like choppin' up driftwood that gets hung up on the landing, mendin' the scow, and such. An' I do a lot of jawin' with the freighters when they're knockin' the icicles off their horses' noses, or checkin' traces and chains—so I know what's goin' on. I hear from one of them he seen my man, and that he got something like the rheumatism so I figger he'll be crawlin' back one day. I sent off for a good German razor and I'm goin' to shave him clean, as I hear now he's got whiskers down to his belt buckle an' I'd sure like to see what he looks like in a bald face."

THE
MIXBLOOD

THE part of him that was Indian paid no attention to the lashing wind that cracked down from the limestone bluffs and whipped the blanket capote against his legs. His Red River cart stood with thirty more on the levee at the foot of Jackson Street in St. Paul, and a distant screeching, heard above the wind, was the fanfare for still more carts coming down the East Road.

He was a Bois Brulé, a half-breed from the Pembina settlements on the border of Canada, 450 miles northwest of the Mississippi River port. His cart, like the others, held the harvest of a

winter's trapping—smoke-dried pelts of muskrat, marten, mink, beaver, fox and sometimes the hide of the rare white wolf.

The cart itself was of remarkable construction, for it was made entirely of wood and not one bit of iron had a part in holding it together. Its timber members were mortised, then bound in green rawhide; even the felloes of the deeply-dished wheels were welded together with rawhide tires. The foot-and-a-half-wide wooden hub, rotating on its greaseless wooden axle, gave out the ear-splitting noise that only a Red River cart could produce.

On the levee, he would trade the skins for the things he needed—traps and gunpowder, blankets and tools, flour, sugar, salt and tea. If the buyers would give him what the furs were worth, perhaps he could afford to bring home a new Hawken rifle and relegate his old Hudson Bay trade gun to the wall pegs, or maybe swap it for a Swedish axe.

But the late March wind sharpened a pang of desire under the sash-bound capote, and the man from the border dismissed the idea of a new rifle. Some bolts of cloth, some bits of jewelry—that would be a better trade on this trip. Up near the junction of the Pembina and the Red River of the North lived a lithe Assiniboine maiden and—well, it was so hurting lonesome most of the time up there.

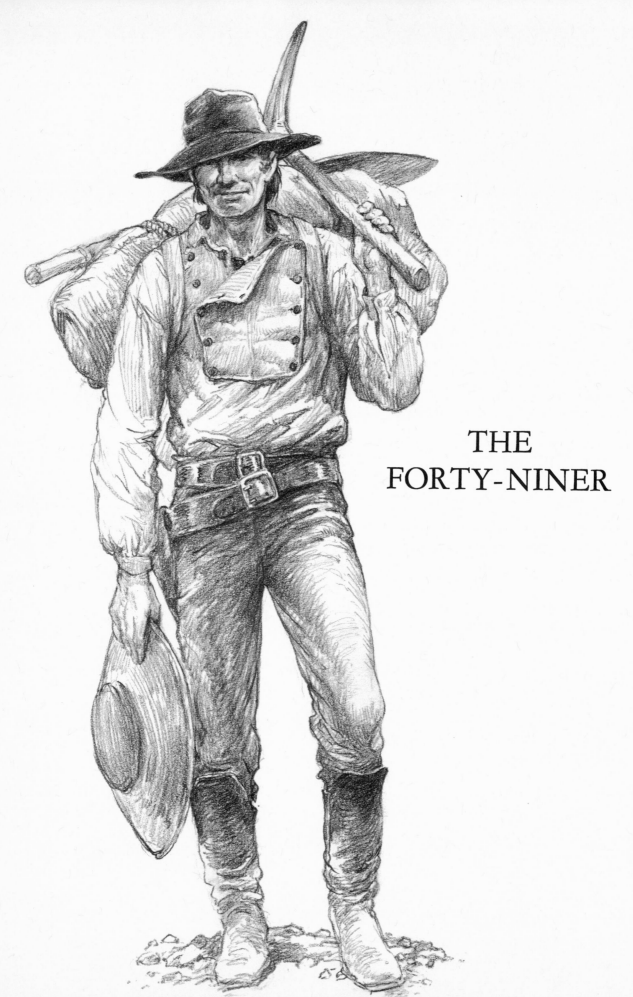

THE
FORTY-NINER

ON THE nineteenth of January, 1848, at Sutter's sawmill in California, James Marshall picked up a little flake of yellow metal, worth probably fifty cents, and started an avalanche of events and legends which is unparalleled in history.

That little speck of gold sent thousands of people scrambling across the continent enduring unbelievable hardships; it sent hundreds of ships, some built specially for the purpose of speed, on 17,000-mile voyages crowded with chafing passengers who were forced to endure one another for thirty weeks. It raised the population of San Francisco from 850 in 1848 to 20,000 in 1849 and added millions on millions to the national treasure.

Men came from everywhere to burrow and scratch for the gold and most of them were strangers to the pick and shovel, pan and rocker. Sailors abandoned their ships, merchants hung placards on their doors proclaiming "Gone to the gold fields," and many a farmer left his new iron plow to rust in a half-turned furrow. At the diggings there were to be found swarthy Mexicans, runaway Negroes, Germans, Frenchmen and Chileans, pigtailed Chinese and muscular Kanakas from Hawaii. The long-jawed Yankee from the Penobscot was there with the rugged boys from Missouri's Pike County, and there were big laughing Australians with their Irish and cockney cousins. Even the Indian came and only he, the native son, seemed out of place.

Raw gold brought sixteen dollars an ounce to its finder and it was but an average claim that could not yield better than that for a day's work. There are records of a seven-man partnership panning as much as 275 pounds in two weeks, and an instance where six and a half ounces were picked out with a pocketknife in thirty minutes.

The rocker made faster work of separating the gold from the gangue than did the pan, but it was a comparatively costly tool even though of crude wooden construction. This rough and simple machine was the forerunner of much mechanical apparatus for getting out the gold, such as steam river-dredges, stamp mills, and a variety of hydraulic mining techniques. But whatever means the miner used to fill his poke, it could not keep pace with the schemes of gamblers, girls, and saloonkeepers who inevitably separated the miner from his gold and sent him back to the Slope.

THE CLAIM JUMPER

THE WHEELWRIGHT

FROM skills inherited from his father as a boy in England, this craftsman kept the wagons of the Western frontier rolling. He had learned the art of the drawknife and spokeshave, of adze and ax, on the tough elm, oak, ash, and beech from which the Sussex farm wagons and carts were fashioned.

The smiths in his father's shop had passed on to him the art of shrinking the hot hoop of iron to the felloes of the dished wheels, and the secrets of drawing out, punching, scarfing, and welding were an added legacy.

Here in a cross-trails town, far removed from the lathes and mortising machinery of the carriage factories, the wheelwright mended broken reaches and axles, replaced spokes and hubs, made new shafts, tongues and hounds, and shimmed the worn brake blocks. To him, the big Conestogas were much like the rural vehicles of Sussex, Wiltshire, and Kent—more spokes, maybe, and a longer bed, but they had a certain kinship in their graceful curves, high wheels, and chamfered timbers. Alone, he could handle most of the repairs arising from the wear and tear of the trail, abetted by the heat, rain, and cold, but to make and set a new tire on a big wheel was when a man needed brawny friends.

It was one of the settlement's interesting hours when the onlookers saw three strong frontiersmen hook the red hot tire from the fire and run with it to the wheel lying bolted through its hub to a platform. One section of the hoop was brought over the felloes and the balance of the circumference was pulled and hammered until it went home amid clouds of choking smoke and orange spurts of flame from the scorching wood. Water was quickly applied from a sprinkling can before the felloes could really burn. Then, like little pistol shots, the sound of the spokes going fully into their mortises from the shrinking and cooling tire gave the wheelwright assurance that he had built a good wheel, with enough dish to resist the smashing lateral motion as well as the three tons of freight that would rest on it over thousands of miles of rutted prairie.

THE GUNSMITH

HERE was a craftsman whose talents were in demand all along the wide frontier. Weapons were a part of almost every man's apparel and, although built ruggedly, inevitable wear or broken parts eventually brought the pieces to the gunsmith's shop.

The smith shown here is clearing the cylinder nipples of a Remington New Model .44 percussion revolver. This gun and the Army Colt of the same calibre were standard side arms of the Union Army, and after the war thousands of these six-shooters went west with the ex-soldiers.

A good gunsmith had a gift for drawing the temper of a newly made spring—a delicate heat-treating operation which left the thin sliver of steel hard but not brittle, tough but flexible. His use of the oilstone could turn a dragging, creepy trigger pull into a crisp, sharp movement and the deft touch of rasp and chisel would bed an action or barrel into the wood precisely.

His vise held, at one time or another, the products of the famous New England firearms factories and numerous smaller shops—the many models of Winchester and Colt, the rugged rifles of Hawken or Sharps, the long handmade Kentuckies, and deadly little derringers, as well as all the "leftovers" of wars from the Revolution to the war with Spain in '98.

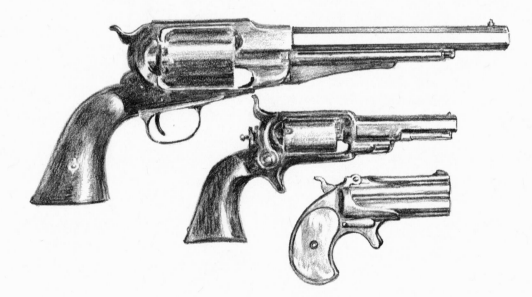

THE CLIPPER'S MATE

THE mate was a calm man and it took a series of outrageous deeds and events to unbalance him. But this bunch —crazy people, a whole shipload of them, with all of their clutter of junk, mostly shovels—had tried him severely, all the way from New York for over ninety days. Many had been ill, others drunk, and some they had to slide over the side, sewed up in a piece of sail-mending canvas. How could sane, reasonable men turn into creatures like this, paying a steep fare to travel the periphery of two continents, just to go scratching for gold in the California hills? They even had the fever showing in their eyes. The lure of gold obsessed them!

The clipper was one of the latest of the long, sharp beauties to slide off the ways in Donald McKay's East Boston shipyard. She carried eight thousand yards of the best canvas on her three masts, and her hollowed bows split the seas like a honed scimitar. The mate loved her and despised the sick treasure-seekers who fouled her decks and cursed her roll.

"In two more days, if the wind holds," he reckoned, "we will dump these gold-mad lunatics at San Francisco." And so it was. In two days the clipper dropped her anchor beyond the scores of abandoned ships that cluttered the harbor, and both passengers and crew went ashore.

Ready for sea, four days later, the captain sent for the supercargo and asked the whereabouts of the ship's mate. Reaching into his waistcoat, the supercargo drew out a small buckskin sack whose contents he spilled out onto the chart table. "I met the mate in a saloon down on the Barbary Coast," he said. "I showed him these nuggets I won at poker from a miner. He got a funny light in his eyes and he went out. Last time I saw him he was going up the street with a shovel on his shoulder."

THE
BLACKSMITH

H E WAS Tubal-cain of the great plains—the ironmaster. He ruled his smoky domain, accompanied by the sound of the squeaking bellows, the ring of hammer on the anvil, the hiss of hot metal dropped into water, the smell of a hot iron shoe on a hoof, the pungent odor of coke in the forge and the acrid stench of charred wood as the tire was set on the felloes or the bands to a hub.

The smith's skill kept the wagons rolling and their teams shod. Horsemen stopped at the smithy to have their ponies' old shoes reset or to get new ones put on at "four bits a foot." Miners brought their single jacks and picks for sharpening. Bullwhackers had their oxen fitted with monad-shaped shoes, their high-sided wagons strapped and plated where the wood surrendered.

He could shape the heavy iron brackets whereon hung the brake beams, or bend inch-thick freighter tires, or beat out an intricate branding iron from a pencil sketch. Sometimes, just for fun, he would take his smallest hammer and a piece of thin metal and on the point of the anvil's bick would fashion a perfect iron rose.

The art of the smith held much of the West together with welds and rivets, brackets and braces, straps and chains.

39

THE RIVER GAMBLER

Among the picturesque people of the Western rivers, the gambler was the most colorful. He was to be found on any of the palatial river boats that plied the Mississippi and the Missouri. His very clothes made his profession evident. A fine beaver top hat rode his head, holding down the generally overlong hair which curled above his high collar. A black stock tie, fastened with a bejeweled horseshoe or other good-luck symbol, was knotted at his throat.

The frock coat of black serge or, in summer, a light-colored one with a black collar, was an especial pride of the gambling gentry. Tight trousers with legs buttoned beneath the instep of polished boots were of cream or checks or stripes.

His shirt would be of finest linen or silk, with either a ruffled or pleated bosom and tightly fitted over this was a gorgeously brocaded vest. He carried a gold or ivory headed cane which more often than not carried a rapier concealed in its core. However, this was not his only armament, for either in the sleeves or the tails of the frock coat, or in the pockets of the fancy waistcoat, he carried a pair of deadly little pistols known as derringers. And then again these might be still further augmented by a six-shooter worn in any convenient place—at hip, underarm, in the hat or waistband.

Cards, dice, wheels, and shells were the usual tools of his trade, but he would lay a bet on anything. Since his floating place of business often engaged in races with other steamboats, this was as exciting a way to win or lose as any more elaborate means of teasing Lady Luck.

There was the well-known story of a steamboat race when the captain crowded on the cordwood so hard that the steam boilers exploded—the safety valves having been weighted down with bags of horseshoes. As the boilers blew up, one gambler shot high by the explosion remarked to another also plummeting skyward. "Bet a thousand I go higher'n you!" "Double it and I'll lay you three to one I'm down first" was the reply.

THE RIVERBOAT CAPTAIN

LOOKING down from the visored pilothouse windows atop the palatial sidewheeler, the captain contemplated the swirling, muddy Mississippi.

This was half a continent away from his home place in Thomaston, Maine, where for generations his people had built and sailed big ocean-going ships. This dirty-brown, two thousand miles of meandering river, unlike the Georges River whose waters were twice daily renewed by the clean, blue tides of Penobscot Bay, was just a wet conglomerate of sloughs, snags, reelfoot lakes and sand bars stretching from oak-covered bluffs to the cane brakes on the delta.

He skippered a vessel whose three-hundred-foot length exceeded that of most ocean carriers and whose progress up and down the river was not dependent on the winds or tides. Forward of her texas house, surmounting the bell, were bolted the coveted antlers—badge of superior speed among the river packets.

He was proud of the many-tubed boilers, topped by crenelated black stacks which, when fed fat pine slabs, could convert river water into that powerful vapor that gave the engines their pulsating life.

The Yankee captain had learned the signs in this tawny ribbon of water: how to suspect a sand bar by the change of surface ripples, how to sense the submerged snag, pointed upstream, whose fang, in a single rip could disembowel the limber hull. For the skipper had been an upper-river pilot— St. Paul to St. Louis—a 625-mile stretch that could make a strong man shudder. It had everything bad—shifting bars, snags, one-way sloughs, the Le Claire rapids, Lake Pepin that was no lake, and the weird illusion of Point No Point, a spit of land that seemingly disappeared on close approach.

Now in winter, he steamed southward on the lower river—twelve hundred miles of combined Missouri and Mississippi and numerous tributaries that joined in the race to the Gulf. This run he knew less well, but expert pilots manned the wheel over the rough stretches.

Memphis, Vicksburg, Natchez, Baton Rouge—all now lay astern—Nine Mile Bend, and then New Orleans! As the packet was being warped to the pilings, the captain's eye caught the distinctive lines of a big square-rigged ship moored off Algiers, across the river. He reached for the long glass, extended its tubes, and felt a hard tug under his brass-buttoned jacket as the lens brought into focus the gold legend on her counter: *Metinicus*, Thomaston, Maine.

HERE were a people unlike all the other pioneers who dreamed of a green paradise in the West, for these sought a land so remote, so unwanted, and desolate that it would excite no one's envy.

Persecution for their beliefs drove them westward from New York State to Missouri by way of Ohio, then back eastward to Illinois where they founded Nauvoo with a population of 15,000, the largest city in Illinois. Their leader, Joseph Smith, was martyred here and his mantle fell on Brigham Young, a rugged man of forty-three years who by nature was remarkably endowed with the talents and instincts of leadership. His people harassed again, Young—inspired by reading the journal of "The Pathfinder," John C. Fremont—abandoned Nauvoo and in the spring of 1846 began the great migration of the Saints to the valley of the Great Salt Lake. He organized series of small bands of emigrants which followed the initial group of two hundred wagons at specified intervals. The first battalion built mills,

THE
MORMONS

shops, and living quarters en route so that succeeding caravans found relatively little difficulty.

The wagon migration continued for five years and as vehicles and draft animals became too expensive, the Mormons resorted to hand-drawn, two-wheeled carts. These were built in Iowa by Mormon carpenters and by September, 1856, a hundred handcarts and nearly five hundred persons arrived at Salt Lake, this group outdistancing every covered-wagon train on the route. That summer two other Mormon brigades headed for Salt Lake, but due to the use of green lumber for the vehicles, the overburdened carts broke down. Of the latter two groups containing a thousand pioneers, 225 died in the trek.

The great congregation of the Church of Jesus Christ of Latter-Day Saints built dozens of towns and communities up and down the valley, and established a self-contained empire which held everything from gristmills and sawmills, farms and ranches, to the great temple and tabernacle which still stand, symbolic of a determined leader and a steadfast people.

THIS was a boy engaged in a dramatic enterprise doomed to last only a little more than a year and a half. The imagination of the nation was captured by the thought of the eighty young riders and their five hundred fast ponies racing endlessly in relays between St. Joseph, Missouri, and Sacramento, California. Between these points they carried the contracted mail at five dollars a half-ounce in a leather *mochila*, with its four locked pockets, slung over a light saddle. It took ten and a half days, which was more than twice as fast as the express stagecoaches could cover the 1,966-mile route.

For a country whose people always craved more and more speed, the Pony Express filled the need for faster communications and moreover was a grand and colorful project. The Kansas freighting company of Russell, Majors and Waddell undertook the gigantic task of establishing the way stations, supplied the stock, hired the riders and hostlers, and put up $100,000 to bring it all about.

As a condition of employment the tough young riders took an oath: "I do hereby swear, before the Great and Living God, that during my engagement, while I am employe of Russell, Majors and Waddell, I will under no circumstances use profane language; that I will drink no intoxicating liquors; that I will not quarrel or fight with any employe of the firm; and that in every respect I will conduct myself honestly, be faithful to my duties, and so direct all my acts as to win the confidence of my employers. So help me God."

Whether all the 'flying horsemen lived up to the oath is doubtful, but carry the mail they did, day and night for eighteen months over scorching deserts and frigid plains, through blizzards and Indian attacks, and around rock slides on the dangerous mountain trails. But a long thin piece of copper wire stretched between telegraph poles brought it all to a sudden end and with it went three-quarters of a million dollars. Left behind was a legend which is as enduring as the mountains the Pony Express riders crossed.

THE
PONY EXPRESS
RIDER

THE HOSTLER

IT WAS mostly a lonely life, here at a relay station on the Butterfield route. But some are made for it. A man can keep fairly busy—feeding and currying the stage relay teams, sewing up some overstrained tugs, maybe building a kettle of soup for the next batch of passengers to come stretching and stamping from the stagecoach.

Those passengers—there were all kinds—complainers, cold ones, hungry ones, nice ones who liked to talk a little, hard ones, and some who used too much redeye booze as an anesthetic against the racking jolts of the mudwagons. Some he saw often, others never again. But they sure relieved the monotony.

The drivers and guards were mostly all business. "Make sure them swing tugs are hooked good" or "Didja fix that collar gall on that nigh wheeler?" Or from the shotgun messenger, "Seen any horsebackers down through here this mornin'?" The mule skinners tooled their jerkline strings up to the corral and unhitched the wagons and trailers. They usually stayed all night and were good company. The freighters that pushed the bull-trains along the route took care of their own critters and slept out under their wagons unless it was cracking cold.

But mostly it was a lonely life out here on the Butterfield route.

THE BULLWHACKER

THE giant of a man, striding beside the plodding six-yoke of draft cattle, was in a cheerful mood. The wheels of his ponderous Studebaker freight wagon and trailer rolled over the gumbo trail toward Deadwood with a steady, satisfying rumble.

Some hours before, however, he was a man of less amiable mien, for he had to ford the Missouri above Fort Pierre and heavy rains to the north had swollen the great river. The familiar marks around the crossing point had been washed away by the ochre torrent. To the near-side wheel ox he said, "A smart kinda fella would jest set here and wait till that muddy crick petered down to natural, but I jest can't, Jumbo. I simply have t' get this load—"

His conversation with the roan ox was interrupted by a thin Indian boy riding up on a paint pony. The boy kneed the pony up to the bearded teamster. "You want take cows and wagons to West River side?" asked the boy.

"Sure do, son, but I can't find the ford and anyhow I think it's too deep. I got stuff in them wagons I don't want wet."

"You walk cows straight, you go right place, water not too much for wagons." "You know the place, son?" the man asked, eyebrows pulled up.

"Know place. Cross over pretty much. My father scout for horse soldiers over there." The boy indicated Fort Pierre across the river with his chin. "You got long rope?"

"Sure," said the teamster. He walked back to the tool box on the front of the wagon and withdrew a hank of tarp lacing. The boy dismounted, took the hank, made an end fast to the doubletree pin on the pole, and proceeded along the chain between the teams of oxen, stringing the rope through the yoke ring of each pair. When he got the line threaded through the ring of the leaders' yoke, he hung the remaining hank on a horn of the oxbow and returned to the man. The boy was on his pony in a bound. "Now," he said,

"I go far in front of cows with rope. You keep rope straight between wagon and me. I go."

So saying, he rode to the head of the bull train, retrieved the rope, rode ahead a bit, tied the hank to the pinto's tail and rode to the river's edge. The man urged his teams down the river bank, their cloven hooves spreading in the mud, and the whole train lined out behind the boy on the pony and into the water. The oxen needed no goad, for the man standing on the wagon-pole directed them by name and the rope was held straight. Through the eddying water they went, following a sand bar, then with mighty lunges dragged the wagons up the bank onto solid ground, floor boards hardly wetted. "We made it, boy," said the teamster. "What a river! Too thin to walk on, too thick to drink!"

THE STAGE DRIVER

THE jehu, up there on the offside of the box, driving the six-horse hitch which hauled the big Concord coach, knew every rock, high-water creek ford, and prairie dog hole on his strip of the Overland Trail. The shiny leather ribbons, arranged through his fingers like the control strings of a puppeteer, telegraphed his every wish and idea to the easy running bays. With lash, brake, and rein, the jehu could maneuver the heavy coach and teams with unbelievable precision over the tawny plains, up pine-covered slopes, and down breathtaking declivities.

He'd worked for Holliday, he'd worked for Adams Express, and now he drew his pay from Wells Fargo. He was at home on a mud wagon, or a mail ambulance, but for style and comfort there was nothing like the handsome stagecoaches built by Abbott Downing up there in New Hampshire. Oh, he got some complaints from passengers already tired out from sitting down for a thousand miles before they got this far. Another jolt, even though the coach body was cradled in the finest bullhide thoroughbraces, would just about drive a bone through flesh that had been completely tenderized anyhow.

Beneath the driver's perch, in the boot, sat the iron-bound treasure chest, the El Dorado of stage robbers—but, shucks, that thing was his seat partner's worry. Drivers are supposed to drive; shotgun messengers are paid to ride herd on gold, money, or whatever valuables are worth the hauling price.

The jehu's day off? Well, now, he usually hired a rig at the livery stable and took himself for a little ride in the country.

THE STAGECOACH BANDIT

AMONG outlaws, the stage robber was a man apart, a strategist, a gambler in a bandanna mask. Courage was something for which he could take no credit—he was born without fear.

He wasn't sitting there, ahorseback in the coulee, as a philanthropic Robin Hood nor an avenging Ben Turpin. No, he was calmly waiting for a certain eastbound stagecoach. Patient research in schedules and choice of personnel had made it fairly certain to be a treasure carrier. That the contents of its rivet-studded box were someone's payroll, or pokes of gold dust grubbed out fleck by fleck, or the hard-won savings of a retired couple—these details bothered him not at all, for his ethics knew no conscience.

Spiraling dust, two miles away, marked the progress of the stagecoach over the sage flat. The trail, due to outcroppings of ledge, was forced to come near the cut bank of the coulee and it was here that the road agent, his Colt poised, would rise from the seemingly empty wasteland.

On the coach, next to its jehu the driver, rode the messenger, eyes squinted beneath a Stetson's brim. Seasoned in the ways of robbers, he watched the brush-rimmed break of the land. A snort and a shying of the lead horses brings the guard's cocked Winchester to bear on the masked figure now appearing over the gray vegetation. A shout of "Hands up, this is a . . ." is cut off by the crash of the rifle, and this time the box rode to Omaha with its lock intact.

THE SHOTGUN MESSENGER

Upon the near side of the swaying Concord's high front seat he sits, gun athwart his knees. From there, the highest point on the high plains, he can see across twenty miles of grass and sage—and it is his business to take a hard look.

Under the leather-cushioned seat, down in the boot, rides the locked treasure box and out there, somewhere, sit the new owners of the box should he fail as guard. Maybe they're not there on this run, or the next, but they'll be along.

The gun, lying there, wearing the wales off his corduroy britches, was often a double-barreled, sawed-off, ten-gauge Greener shotgun—whence came the messenger's sobriquet. Sometimes the weapon was a lever gun, a Winchester 44-40, a much better piece for long range, and on his hip was the old plow-handled .44 Colt six-iron. One belt of cartridges, containing the same fodder for both rifle and revolver, girdled his middle.

When the road agents rise from some gully, he knows that the first shot must be his and it must tally a bulls-eye, for there is no encore in this deadly game of "who-gets-the-box."

THE SHEEPHERDER

A RAW wind swept up the flank of the mountain, but the swarthy man ignored its frigid blast as he pried at the interlocked rock fragments to enlarge and deepen a rectangular cavity in the earth with the blade of a camp shovel.

Thirty years before, this Basque shepherd had traded his birthplace in the Pyrenees for this mountainland in the New World, the lonely Bighorns. Descendant of a unique race whose origin and language are still unknown, he followed in the footprints of conquistadores now dimmed by the passing of three centuries. He came not to search for the treasure of Cibola's seven cities, nor had he the lust for conquest that drove his countryman Coronado across the southern plains. No, the man came to do what he did best, to tend sheep in the high mountain pastures.

The excavation had now reached proportions which satisfied the man and he dropped the shovel. He went over to the side of the camp wagon and picked up an object wrapped in a worn-out blanket. Three sheep were standing by the mound of rock and soil when he returned with his burden and to them he said, "You come to pay respects. I think you know if it were not for Carléts you would be the ones I bury today. The wolves are now dead too, but Carléts will never know it and I shall never have a dog like him again."

THE PEDDLER

To THE ears of a pioneer's wife, a certain clinking and rattle from an odd wagon was more a harbinger of spring than the chirp of a robin.

As soon as the trails were fit for travel the smiling Syrian, up on his perch over the wagon box, brought the world's wares right to her leather-hinged door. The collection of utensils, notions, yard goods, trinkets, tools, sewing sundries, shoes, cutlery, window glass, lamps and wicks, books, writing paper and pens—it was to her truly a merchandise fair, an exposition on wheels.

The peddler, like every merchant on the frontier, had his ups and downs. He started the trade route to his widely scattered customers with a pack on his back and a bulging, many-pocketed overcoat. Then he dealt in small articles such as thread, needles and pins, buttons, scissors, knives and razors, lampwicks, and a few patent pills and salves.

These days, he carried objects of more bulk and of much greater variety, for the load was pulled by a tractable span of mules which spared his feet and back.

He disliked thinking about the first pair of mules he owned and his first wagon. It was years ago, but memories of those beasts still nettled him. The peddler had paused one day at an auction of livestock and equipment in a prairie town. An offering that appealed to his Syrian ancestry was a pair of medium-sized brown mules and he won the bid. He also acquired a light spring wagon and a set of harness in good condition. He mounted the seat, clucked to the team, and moved down the road at a nice pace. The peddler was pleased and many good merchandising ideas were marinating in his agile mind.

The mules came to a little stream and stopped short of the water. The peddler clucked with gusto, but they didn't stir. He tried some pure Damascus invective, vituperation that would ordinarily catapult the most reluctant dromedary from Damascus to Samarkand, but there was no progress. He belabored the asinine rumps with a stick; they brayed, but move they did not.

In desperation, he gathered some tumbleweed and great dry tufts of prairie grass and set these combustibles under the mules. "You'll move now, you long-eared offspring of some sway-backed, ill-begotten jenny!" he remarked unpleasantly as he scratched a match on the sole of his boot and touched off the conflagration. The mules moved ahead. But just far enough to put the wagon squarely over the burgeoning fire!

But that was quite a long while ago, and maybe it should be laughed at now—just a little and not too loudly.

IN THE sere hills of the Southwest and in its hot arid flatlands, he was truly a desert rat, but in the cool canyons of the Rockies and the deep cut gulches of the Black Hills he was more properly called a prospector. In the years after the great California gold rush, hundreds of lone men roamed unfrequented regions which few other than the native Indians had ever seen. They searched unceasingly for that bit of "color" which would indicate the bonanza waiting at the end of the prospector's rainbow—and a few found it.

Most of these men grew gray and old in their wanderings and with the years acquired a knowledge of geology and mineralogy which was more instinct than learned science. With his burro packed with the camping gear and his few hand tools, the prospector picked and poked in fissured and eroded arroyos of brown, iron-stained rock where the gold was freed from its associated sulphides as they oxidized and weathered away. Sometimes he worked the stream beds with his shovel and pan. The heavier nuggets concentrated in the rills and he learned that the more rounded the gold specimens became, the farther they had traveled from the mother lode.

The desert rats did not ignore other metallic ores but there was a fascination in seeking for gold, a fascination which made the actual finding of the precious metal something of an anticlimax.

THE
DESERT RAT

THE KIDS

YOUNGSTERS of the frontier were subject to sounds, sights, and smells that, in most places, are now scarce.

A favorite hangout was at the wide door of the blacksmith shop, where the clang and clank of metal being shaped on the anvil was a wonderful sound, as was the hissing and smell of a hot horseshoe being cooled suddenly in a tub of water.

The bell and whistle of the fast mail train steaming into town dragged small boys (and big boys), like a baggage hook, to the depot platform. The shouts of men and the bawling of cattle at the corrals farther down the track took them to a perch on a rail near the loading chutes.

"When I grow up" ambitions varied with the moment. The engineer of the locomotive or the stage driver who had just pulled up his coach to meet the train were high on the list of vocations. The lanky sheriff with his bone-handled gun and nickel star had his admirers, and a particularly talented bronco buster was a hero at rodeo time.

However, another ten years packed behind the huck shirt and stovepipe pants generally transformed the hero-worshipers into storekeepers, ranchers, carpenters or, now and then, a solemn minister.

THE HORSE TRADER

To PLAY the game of horse-swapping successfully for profit, one had need of more than a gift for discerning equine faults and virtues. The horse trader needed to be just as much a judge of men and how to play upon their urge for possession.

He knew the tricks—how to float the corner teeth to resemble a younger mouth, to work a bit of dye into neat dapples to darken the hide of a whitening mule, and how to show a nearly blind pony. Sometimes even he was outdone, for there were ways of gradually doping a skinny nag with arsenic so that on trading day he was round and fat, with shining hair and a good appetite. But the true state of affairs would become obvious some days later when the animal, deprived of the arsenic, would revert to a dull-eyed skeleton in a lackluster coat, with no interest in fodder.

Seldom did the trader make an even swap, horse for horse. He liked something "to boot." If it wasn't a twenty dollar bill, a set of harness thrown in could conclude a deal, or maybe a couple of heifers or some pigs.

Traders enjoyed outdoing one another, as both participants in a deal knew the law of "caveat emptor" and the loser in the transaction lived for the day when he could even the score.

THE DOCTOR

A BAY gelding hitched to a certain coal-box buggy before a lantern-lit shack could be an indication of dire trouble, or sometimes it betokened only the birthday of a six-pound plainsman.

Usually, the midnight ride by the frontier doctor was preceded by a shout from a boy on a farm horse under the office window. "Doc, come quick! Ma's breathin' awful funny!"

The self-reliant pioneers could patch up run-of-the-mill abrasions, contusions, and cuts, mix up various nostrums for colds, aches, and pains, and apply poultices of odoriferous substance for drawing infections. But there came a time when these did not avail, and the inevitable trip for the doctor ensued.

Probing for and extracting bullets became a routine operation, and neat lacings of catgut reunited flesh parted by a Bowie knife, the patient generally anesthetized by overdoses of sour-mash whiskey when the chloroform ran out.

He served also as dentist, coroner, pharmacist, and, if pressured enough, as a veterinarian. And he could do a creditable bit of sculpture in plaster of Paris over the splints which joined a cowboy's fractured tibia. Often as not, his bill was paid by a "Thanks, Doc. Now, if I can ever do anything for you—"

THE VIGILANTES

WHERE the law seemed slow to act and the punishment less than equal to the crime, impatient citizens formed secret groups to expedite matters.

These Vigilance Committees sprang up whenever the lawless element became too numerous or their depredations and murders too frequent. A rap of a six-shooter's butt on the door or the crash of a sawed-off shotgun's barrels through a windowpane preceded a quick ride for the malefactor to any tall object that would serve as a gibbet. Trees, porch rafters, barn eaves, corral gateposts, and even flagpoles and church steeples lent their height to shorten a life.

The vigilantes held no true court; they carried out only the decrees of "Judge Lynch" and his hempen justice. The crack of a rawhide quirt on his horse's rump was the last earthly sound the doomed man heard before he swung into eternity. The victim was left hanging there as a reminder to those with easy consciences not to steal, cheat, or murder in that vicinity.

But, when the anonymous horsemen rode off, the buzzards that had been waiting in the brassy sky wheeled down to join in the final obsequies for the swaying corpse, watched by the horse that had innocently helped to break his master's neck.

THE GRADER

A BIG red-faced Irishman strode at the same pace as his team of bay Percherons, and their trace chains stiffened into solid bars as the fresno scraper's blade bit deep into the red gravel and filled its eighteen-cubic-foot maw. The rein ends hung around his neck, for he needed his hands to tilt the load and dump it at the head of the fill. The scraper alone weighed three hundred pounds and, with its scoop packed with over 1,900 pounds of earth, it was a mighty feat to start its lift and roll out its contents in the right spot. But this he did with perspiring regularity, ten hours a day. At sunset, when he pulled the collars and hames from the Percherons, 225 yards of earth had been moved from here to there.

He was a grader, pushing through the roadbed for the Union Pacific, and his work was usually located many miles in advance of the track layers. Sometimes when logs for ties and bridge trestles or cordwood for locomotive fuel was in short supply he worked his teams up into the timber country and hauled the hundred-foot pine trunks down to the right of way.

Unlike most of the graders, he was not a hard drinker. The story is told that one evening he drove his team into one of the "hell-on-wheels" towns that preyed on the railroad workers, and went into a saloon, a bucket swinging from his calloused fist. "Fill this up," he said as he handed it over the bar. He took the beer-filled growler from the bartender and went out to his team at the hitchrail and gave the offside bay the entire pailful. He returned and had the bucket re-filled, then went out and regaled the nearside horse. He returned to the bar and asked, "An' what be I owin' ye?" The bartender said, "Well first, friend, how about one for yourself?" "Oh no," said the grader. "I couldn't do that, y' know, I'm drivin'!"

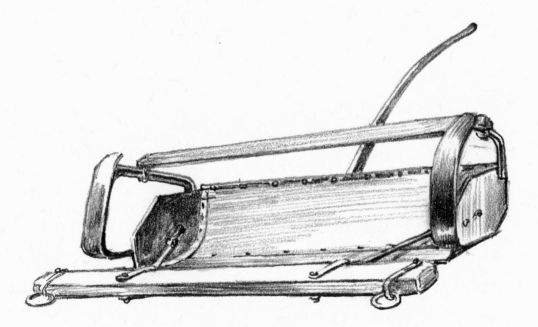

THE term "rustler" was applied to a person who was excessively care-free in his manner of appropriating other people's horses and cattle, especially the latter.

Rustling was practiced over a long period, even after the end of the frontier era. In many instances cattle stealing was carried on to build up a shoestring herd, and in other cases the thieves butchered the stolen animals and sold the beef to the railroad construction gangs then laying the tracks that would link the East with the Pacific.

A rustler who was adept at changing brands was called a "brand artist." His art lay in the use of a hot running iron, a hooked iron rod with which he could make alterations. A "brand blotter" was a name signifying that the rustler used the technique of running an iron over a whole brand and blurring the marking. The resulting scar made it very difficult to read, unless the animal in question were slaughtered, after which the original brand could then be deciphered from the inside of the hide. If apprehended with a running iron in his possession, a person suspected of rustling was considered guilty and the sentence of death by the noose was carried out promptly.

There is an old story about running iron work that was added to the I C brand. The ranchman owning that mark noticed that some of the steers in his herd had brands reading I C U. Realizing that there was rustling afoot, the rancher roped the animals with the excess letter and added another character to the brand. It now read I C U 2!

THE
RUSTLER

THE
CAVALRYMAN

Hᴀʀᴅ-ʀɪᴅɪɴɢ, tough as a quirt, with a vocabulary so iridescent and corrosive it could tarnish the bronze of his saber hilt—this was the frontier horse soldier.

Why would a man endanger his life, live in wretched barracks, eat food that was scarcely palatable, and exist under rigid discipline for a five-year hitch, all for forty cents a day?

Like the African outposts of the French Foreign Legion, the widely spaced frontier forts of the West were a sanctuary to many a wanted man. Some recruits joined the service from some misguided idea of glory and adventure spawned by lurid dime novels. Others enlisted because there was simply no other job, this being a time of frequent depressions. Still others were ex-soldiers caught in the uncertain aftermath of the Mexican and Civil wars.

Perhaps the risks were not quite as high as is commonly believed, for in the course of 1,240 battles with the Indians, 1,105 men were killed, which averages out to less than one death per fight. But the long marches—one of dragoons, for instance, which covered 2,200 miles in 99 days— were enough to kill men of iron, and the horses they rode were not the well-mannered equines of the tended bridle path but indifferent cavalry mounts worth about $60 but for which the remount contractor collected $125 from the government.

Despite all the privations and handicaps, by the time the twentieth century dawned, the horse soldier of the army in the West had subdued the finest light cavalry in the world, that of the American Indian.

THE
SWAMPER

Usually, he was only a butt for rough jokes and crude jibes, a colorless little man of menial tasks around the paneled and mirrored saloon. He mopped the floor, polished the mahogany woodwork, burnished the brass cuspidors, and cleaned the chimneys of the hanging lamps.

Before coming to San Francisco's Barbary Coast, the swamper had been a cook's louse on many roundups and had walked numberless miles alongside a chuckwagon gathering bits of firewood to fill the cowskin fuel bin which swung beneath the wagon.

His broken boots and shabby clothing were hand-me-downs and he owned little of the world's goods. The swamper's most prized belongings were an old buffalo-hide coat and a Schofield pattern Smith and Wesson revolver. The latter he had found along a railroad track where it had most likely bounced from the holster of a cavalry trooper on track patrol.

On this frosty night the head bartender had sent the little swamper for coal oil to fill the reservoirs of the lamps. As he elbowed his way back through the batwing doors, an oil can in each hand, he accidentally jostled a departing patron, a man who held a wide reputation as a gunfighter and was possessed of an evil temper.

With a curse, the man spun on his high heels, grabbed the apologetic swamper by the lapels of his old buffalo coat which, splitting down the back, came away in two halves. The angered gunfighter snatched up one of the fallen oil cans and, with the ruins of the swamper's coat, strode across the snowy plank walk to the gutter where he tossed the coat and poured oil on it. He rasped his thumbnail on the head of a lucifer match and in an instant the swamper's pride was in flames. With a crooked grin, the gunfighter turned to the little man, saying, "Now, Swampy, you got some light to see who you're bumpin' into!"

Without reply, the swamper walked slowly through the populous saloon to his tiny room at the rear. In a moment he returned, a big Schofield six-shooter hanging loosely in his bony hand. The curious crowd watched as he approached the gunfighter who had re-entered the bar room. "What now, you clumsy runt? Figurin' on shootin' me with that thing?" said the man, as he toyed with a gill of liquid courage.

"No, sir," said the swamper, "but I'd like to show you what'd happen if I did."

He flicked the gun hammer to full cock, pulled the trigger, and a neat hole appeared in a calendar on the wall. "Now," the little man said, "I'll bet this Schofield pistol against that nice alpaca coat you're wearin' that I can put the rest of the slugs in this gun through that same bullet hole."

"It's a bet, Swampy, shoot."

The reports of the detonating cartridges came so close together the sound was a continuous roar and every eye was on the calendar as the blackpowder smoke cleared. There was but one neat hole!

Later that night the head bartender ambled his heavy frame to the tiny room at the rear where the swamper fondled his new alpaca coat. "Tim, that was the most wonderful shooting I've ever seen. How'd you ever learn to handle a gun like that?"

"Oh, shucks, boss, that was nothin'. I just fired one bullet. All the other shots were blanks."

THE
TRAIN ROBBER

THE engineer peered out from the cab of the leaning engine as it rounded a curve and his hand suddenly stiffened on the throttle. There was something burning on the track! He cut off the steam, then hit the brake valve hard, and as the compressed air pushed the brake shoes against the spinning tires a great cascade of orange sparks circled the drive wheels and shot rearwards down the rails.

A pile of flaming ties lay crisscrossed on the track and the cowcatcher nearly parted them as the locomotive came to a wheel-flattening stop, vapor hissing from the steam chests and safety valves.

Coming from behind a grove of cottonwoods, a rider spurred a nervous buckskin horse up to the noisy engine and, with a cocked carbine, wordlessly motioned the engineer and his fireman down from the cab. The horseman herded them past the tender, down half the length of the express car where, at its barred side door, he reined up the buckskin.

"Now, boys, I don't like to hurt you or bother the passengers. All I want is for the express joker in there to hand me a sack addressed to the Colorado Territorial Bank. You tell him that!" The engineer relayed the order through the small aperture which appeared when the door slid back a trifle. There was no argument from within and in a moment or two the opening widened and a labeled canvas sack was handed out to the man on the buckskin. He felt the sack over carefully, then said, "All right, now I'll ride behind you two to the engine. In case there is any funny business with guns from that express hombre—well, let's just not have any nuisance!"

At the step he motioned the engine crew back aboard and said pleasantly, "Sure do appreciate your cooperation." Then, slinging the sack by its drawstring to the saddle horn, he spun the buckskin and started for the cottonwoods.

The robber had ridden no more than five horselengths when an ear-splitting shriek came from the locomotive as the fireman hauled down on the whistlecord. The buckskin horse went straight up, forehooves pawing the air, and the robber was catapulted from the saddle, along with the carbine and money sack. When the robber wakened, the engineer was standing over him, holding the carbine, and the fireman was remarking to the buckskin, "Sure do appreciate your cooperation."

THE GUNFIGHTER

HERE was a character of the Old West who spawned an infinity of folklore and legend. His prowess with the six-shooter and the fabulous speed of his draw have been embellished and magnified out of all proportion.

In a region where most of the population was armed, a few men would be singled out as exceptionally talented in the use of firearms. This skill had a market value, for it could be employed in enforcement of law, or bartered for purposes that ranged all the way from guarding gold on a stage run to outright assassination.

It was an unwritten law that whoever was first to draw his gun was liable for the consequences of a gunfight. The gunfighter, by his superior swiftness at the draw and accurate marksmanship, had a legal excuse for manslaughter when he said, as he pointed to his prostrate opponent, "He drew first"—thus proclaiming the fact that the shooting was done in self-defense.

Many devices were employed to gain a millisecond of time, that interval being the difference between life or death. The single-action revolver was the subject of much experiment and alteration, as this type of side arm was in high favor and its strong lock-work could be precisely adjusted, then honed to an acme of smoothness.

Many gunfighters filed off the front sight to prevent it from catching the lips of the holster and often sawed off the barrel so that its length would clear the leather faster. Another trick was to remove the front of the trigger guard so that the forefinger could find the trigger with no obstruction. Sometimes the trigger was removed entirely and the gun was then fired by slipping the hammer from the thumb.

The holster was arranged according to the whims of its wearer, often hanging low on the thigh, so that the gun hand naturally brushed the pistol butt. Some scabbards were altered by taking out either front or rear stitching and a spring was installed to clasp the gun by its cylinder. There was a form of swivel holster from which the revolver was not drawn but fired through the open bottom. The gunfighter brought his hand down on the butt, tilting the gun up and thumbing back the hammer simultaneously. This one worked well with the slip-hammer technique.

Gunfighters practiced incessantly and their movements became reflexes. A case in point involved the fabled Wild Bill Hickok. It is said that Hickok, this once, sat with his back to the door while playing cards in Number 16, a popular saloon in Deadwood's main street. One Jack McCall came into the place and, drawing a gun, shot the famous gunfighter in the back of the head. Hickok died instantly, but legend has it that when he was picked up from the floor, his six-shooters were in his hands!

Incidentally, the cards Wild Bill was holding were aces and eights, and to this day that combination is called "The Dead Man's Hand."

THE
HARD-ROCK MINER

BURIED beneath an overburden of clay, rock, hardpan, talus, or quicksand lay hidden the raw ores and veins of precious metals. These occurred in many localities across the world, but tales of the fabulous treasure of the Far West has brought Janos thousands of miles from his beloved Danube. His skills—gained in the Hungarian mines—are pitted against the tough rhyolite and dolomite of the New World, but mostly it is a matter of a powerful back, a pair of muscular arms, and blister-proof calloused hands which wield the drill and sledge, the pick and shovel and hopefully will uncover the ancient pocket in which lies the silver or gold lode.

After the long journey, over Europe and the wide Atlantic and across broad America, Janos' pocketbook is thin, so for a long time he must dig the treasure to fill another man's strongbox. But some day, some good day . . . yes—he saw a place about twenty miles away, up a canyon, which might hide the fortune, the one that would again fatten the lean purse.

THE MARSHAL

A NICKELLED badge on his vest—that was about all that made him look different from the other citizens. Almost everybody had some kind of gun draped from a cartridge belt that circled their hips, so that wasn't any mark of distinction.

But if you looked harder, there was something else. His eyes—sure, that was it. The eyes were a hard brown, like old briar roots, with black, pin-sharp pupils—keen umber eyes that flicked over the length of the street with the speed of a snake's tongue. And another thing—he kept his back to a wall or a post.

He had a reputation as a town tamer, up in the tough Kansas trail towns and in mean places in the panhandle of Texas. People got shot and some of them died. Other people, friends of the dead ones, griped about these gunfights, so they'd come looking for a chance to even things for their dear dead friends. They'd build themselves into a legend for having plugged a town-taming, quick-shot marshal. Some of these people would stoop to bushwhacking, backshooting, sneak shots. So the marshal leaned against walls and things, when they were handy, and kept his coattails clear of his six-shooter, and flicked briar-brown eyes over the street, and stayed alive.

THE ENGINEER

THE gleaming new rails of the St. Paul & Pacific Railroad arrowed westward from St. Paul, over the prairies beyond the Mississippi, to the buffalo plains of Dakota, through the Badlands, on to the shining mountains and beyond.

On a straight run over the steel trail, the locomotive "William Crooks" thundered toward Minot, bit in its teeth, and its proud engineer savored the hot metallic odor as it clicked over the rail joints at seventy miles an hour. His was a justifiable pride, for unlike the two-mile-an-hour gait of his father's teams twenty years before over this same terrain, the great iron horse snorted in a tireless pace past the old landmarks that he dimly recalled.

He was a sort of hero when he tooled the engine into the depot. Small boys were awed that one man could control the shining monster with such aplomb, and even their fathers felt a twinge of envy as the engineer brought the great engine to a gentle stop, heat waves dancing over the blue Norway iron lagging of its boiler front.

Yep, that beautiful 4-4-0 was the fastest thing on wheels in the whole west and Pete, the engineer, was one proud Swede.

THE BOUNTY
HUNTER

HERE was a man nobody really loved. Hungry for gold, but having no taste for the business end of a shovel, his ambition was fired by the dollar signs on the reward posters which were conspicuously displayed across the wide land.

His peculiar talents for tracking, eavesdropping, and perseverance were his forte. Once on the trail of a fugitive, the bounty hunter was like an ever-following shadow over desert and plain, in the dives and dens of the frontier towns, up in the lonely hills and along the river courses. Sometimes his outlaw quarry knew of his relentless follower and laid false trails; sometimes he would try to ambush his nemesis from a rocky crag or from a narrow defile through the rimrock.

Usually the bounty hunter won the grim contest—descending on the luckless man in some hinterlands hideout and taking him, as the wanted poster proclaimed, "DEAD OR ALIVE" for $500. As the specifications stated, the reward was payable for the prisoner in either condition, and the hunter often chose the former, for a man could sleep at night when packing back only a carcass.

THE story of saddles and saddle making runs back to antiquity and the types of saddles for various animals and the uses to which they were put are numberless.

The early saddles of the frontier were devoid of much of the trimmings of a later day. They consisted of a "saddletree," a frame fashioned of tough wood and covered with rawhide. The saddle had most of its components exposed, skeleton fashion, and if its many extrusions proved uncomfortable a *mochila* or leather housing went over the whole structure with only the horn and cantle protruding through slits and holes.

The saddlemaker was a good woodcraftsman. On his choice of wood and the sculpturing of the saddletree depended the strength and form-fitting qualities. The weather side was carved to roughly conform to the human anatomy and its underside was a negative mold of the animal's back. Early saddles had no lining but were buffered by a heavy double blanket cinched under the tree. In later times sheepskin liners were added, plus a variety of other embellishments such as skirts, jockeys, fenders, cantle rolls, double *cinchas, tapaderos* covering the stirrups, and deep embossing and carving in the heavy skirtings.

The shape of the fork, that part which bridged the horse's withers, underwent much modification, the earliest rigs having what was called a slick fork. Toward the end of the frontier era, the saddle had made quite a marked departure in design from its Spanish and Mexican prototypes—the fork was so deeply undercut as to nearly clasp the rider's thighs, the thinned-down horn was fortified with steel instead of the prominent wooden apple-horn or Mexican saucer.

The saddlemaker also made packsaddles, and designed harness for many uses, from fine breast-collar rigs for light buggies to heavy bullhide-covered chain harness for teams hauling ore wagons or dragging a scoop scraper.

THE
SADDLEMAKER

THE SOD BUSTER

MAYBE he came from Missouri when his old well gave out, or maybe off a patch of played-out red dirt somewhere east of the Appalachians. Anyhow, now he's here—wife, plow, and mule, too.

It's going to be rough, this first year or so. The roots of the buffalo grass have built a tough turf mantle a thousand years old and they are mean to split into a furrow. But if the mule doesn't founder, and the plow and beam stay together, and the rain comes sometimes, he's got a place on the frontier he can call home, for this is good soil.

THE MECHANIC

Even in its infancy, the frontier cried loudly for men who could build and repair machinery and mechanical contrivances, for these men were rare anywhere and particularly so beyond the Mississippi.

For years, waterwheels and windmills had powered gristmills and sawmills, and the construction and maintenance of these crude machines was not a highly technical endeavor, as compared with the building and care of exotic engines introduced by the age of steam.

But now there were locomotives, traction engines, riverboats, and all sorts of stationary and portable engines harnessed to the energy of steam. Behind these wonderful machines was a man who understood the mysterious power that moved the pistons in the cylinders. His was a strange world of boilers and pressure gauges, valves and ports, of intakes and exhausts, cranks and connecting rods, flywheels, governors, and eccentrics.

With this unique knowledge and a delicate use of valve and wrench, the mechanic coaxed the mixture of fire and water to turn the paddle wheels, pump the wells, thresh the wheat, hoist the logs, drive the trains, and to do, with speed and ease, a hundred other chores impossible for mere men and horses.

THE RANCHER'S WOMAN

FOR a time, she was simply the wife of a ranchman—cooking, cleaning, washing, mending, and sharing in his worries and triumphs, being mother to his sons. Then, suddenly, it was different. One afternoon the twisted horns of a loco steer had instantly changed her into a widow and deprived her boys of a father.

But that was long ago. Now, at seventy, she still runs the spread at a profit. When problems arise that her sons can't fathom, she solves them from the

seat of a buckboard, her old Frazer saddle stiffened and gathering dust in the shed.

In the early evening, though, she sits, hands folded, in the rocker her man made a half century before. She looks out at the buttes, and the mountains beyond. Then, from nowhere, she seems to hear a familiar husky voice, "Woman, you have done a good job of work."

THE BARTENDER

Whether he ruled a domain fronted by paneled and polished mahogany or presided over a plank supported by kegs, his establishment was Mecca to the nomads of the prairies and mountains.

Seldom was the bartender of the frontier called upon to concoct an exotic mixture, his stock in trade being whiskey, brandy, and beer, the first two poured uncut and with potency undiluted from the bottle.

But more than dispenser of spirits, he was the confidant of the lonely, a relayer of messages, an information bureau, a lost-and-found depot, and referee to many a quarrel.

Early saloons of the Old West varied from a quickly set up plank bartop in a tent or a shack to a mobile barroom on flanged wheels rolling along as the advancing ribbons of steel brought the railroad over the plains. When the towns became established a more elaborate structure housed the shrine of Bacchus, complete with batwing doors, hardwood bar, and a long mirror. The latter was the pride of the place, for it had to be carefully packed and hauled in a big freight wagon over a thousand miles of jolts, hub-splitting ruts, and rocks.

Though noise and hilarity were earmarks of a drinking emporium, when things got out of reason or the great mirror's unity was threatened, a well-placed cranial tap from a bung starter could restore order. If matters were getting to the riot stage, the sawed-off scattergun kept under the bartop was an awesome compellent to decorum, its twin barrels preserving the peace.

THE LAWYER

COWTOWN lawyer! That wasn't exactly the future he saw for himself back in law school at Harvard under the great legal teachers, Story and Greenleaf. The unexpected inheritance of a frame building had decided where his shingle was now nailed. So here he sat, a newly framed law degree on the wall, a set of secondhand law books shelved beneath it.

In this dusty, bovine metropolis most minor disagreements had been quickly adjudicated by fists, and serious ones were discharged in one of the six chambers of "Judge Colt." But a kind of creeping civilization had begun sifting over the rangelands and the reasoning citizens began to question the fairness of decisions reached by the force of the uppercut or the speed of the draw.

So if the frontier had reached the age of reason, it had made a place for the law, and here was as good a spot as any to put the law to work, the lawyer figured. The clink of spur rowels on the porch heralded his first client.

Hᴇ ʀᴇᴀʟʟʏ was a jewel, but to hear it from him, you'd think the only compliments for his excellent cooking were the ones relating to the high potency of the carbolic acid in the coffee.

Gimpy, they call him now. Time was when he could stand pretty square on two bowed legs, but that was before a wall-eyed, equine outrage mangled a knee on the corner-sticks of a corral. So he was no bronc fighter anymore, no ten-dollar-a-head buster. He was that rare creature, a really good cook.

He managed a rolling kitchen—the chuck wagon and its four-horse team. On the roundup, this wagon was a storehouse for the food and the utensils for its preparation, the bedrolls and warsacks of the cowboys, and various tools. It had bows to hold up a tarpaulin and a braced shelf on the side for the water keg. In place of a tail gate was a compartmented box with a bottom-hinged lid that made a table when opened out and its prop leg was swung down and latched.

Gimpy was practically a chef, compared to the grab-bag pot-slingers of most cow outfits. He could conjure up a pan of sourdough biscuits, light, fluffy and golden-domed, that were better than most peoples' grandmothers could bake. His stews were delectable, and highly acclaimed out of his earshot, and there was never a morsel left over when he created a dried apple

THE
WAGON COOK

pie or built something wonderful out of a tin of canned cherries.

In a flour-sack apron, Gimpy would stand there by his fire looking from sunburned face to face as the cowhands consumed what he provided. From them no praise would be forthcoming—not in words—but the rhythmic cadence of masticating mandibles spoke in superlatives their esteem for his effort. Of course, when all the dishes had been put into the "wreck pan" under the wagon, some chaparejoed gourmet would stroll over and commence conversationally, "Wal, now Gimp, about thet chemistry you call java—"

THE LADY
OF THE SALOON

SHE was still a pretty woman—not nearly as hard as the liquor she served, or as cold as the beer, nor was she as tough as the joint she owned. Her last name was Hennessey and she had hair the color of cognac, so it was quite natural that her sobriquet was Brandy.

She was once married to an officer of cavalry, a most devoted mate, but an inveterate gambler. Off duty, there was little to do on this bleak Dakota post but to play at poker and in this diversion he was an expert. To while away the winter nights he taught his wife the game and how to detect a stacked deck and to discern a crooked deal.

Then, one day in May, to the stirring strains of *Garryowen*, her officer in full battle gear rode away with his troop, following a reckless, long-haired general.

Weeks later a dusty courier, on a lathered cavalry horse, rode through the gates of Fort Abraham Lincoln and told the terrible story of the massacre at the Little Big Horn. Brandy, bitter with grief, packed a few belongings and in company of other bereaved wives, left the fort for a Missouri River landing where they boarded a southbound sidewheeler.

To forget the recent past, Brandy played poker with a group of passengers, but in a few hours lost her stake. She left the card table and went down the deck to the stateroom of one of the ladies from the fort.

"Louise," she pleaded, "please let me have a hundred dollars. I'll repay you tomorrow."

The next morning when the poker game resumed, Brandy was again seated at the baize-covered table and by noon she had won a great sum of money and acquired the deed to a Montana saloon.

She rapped on the door of her friend's stateroom and, upon being admitted, extended two hundred dollars and remarked, "Thank you, Louise, here's your money and some interest it earned this morning!"

"But, Brandy, how could . . ."

"It was simple. Those crooks in there whipsawed everybody they could entice into the game. I lost my money learning their tricks, so last night I went to the purser and told him I needed some cards for a party and he sold me five decks, all that he had, in fact. I sat up all night marking and resealing the packs.

"This morning before the game commenced I went back to the purser and told him my party didn't come off and that I'd like to sell the cards back at half price. He bought them and I went to the salon where the game was just starting. I played a few hands, then complained about the poor condition of the cards. One of the gamblers sent for the purser and bought two decks. . . . As I said, Louise, it was fairly simple."

THE
COWBOY

WHOLE forests have been cut down to supply the pulp for the paper on which the endless story of the American cowboy has been printed. It seems strange—at first—that stories of such a workaday job and, in general, a hard and dirty one, should command an insatiable interest, not only to Americans but to readers throughout the world.

The cowboy was a legend even when the cattle trails were newly blazed. Perhaps there was something that fired the imagination about a handful of young men who took great herds of half-wild cattle over inhospitable terrain with innumerable dangers for hundreds and even thousands of miles. The cowboy was a sort of centaur in chaps. Armed with the ubiquitous revolver and with the long-reaching loop of his lariat, he seemed invincible. Even the horse he was part of, and his saddle—which was both storehouse and workbench—were different from their counterparts in other cattle-raising countries.

The geographical and topographical background of the cowboy's legend, too, painted a backdrop for the drama that was quite unmatched in variety, for it covered half a continent. There were deserts, and plains, foothills, high mountains and rolling prairies, canyons, buttes and mesas, rivers and rimrock. The vegetation changed with the latitude and altitude; it varied from the desert saguaro and Joshua trees, to mesquite, yucca and sotol. On the high plains, sagebrush and tumbleweed, buffalo grass and greasewood ochred and grayed the scene. Then, in the mountains, came the tall stands of trees, both evergreen and hardwood, and in the high reaches above the timber, the exquisite alpine growth.

All this gave rise to a myriad of situations which formed the fabric of the episodes in the life of the cow-country people. With a seasoning of wild animals, Indians, recalcitrant horses and stampeding cows, privations, exciting modes of transportation, gold strikes, border incidents and wars, the development of firearms and expert uses thereof—it made a colorful kaleidoscope of adventurous action.

The cowboy's story, though so often told, was nevertheless but one part of a greater drama—life on the American frontier.

As DANGEROUS as fused guncotton awaiting the match, an unruly, shouting mob surged in the dusty street before the county jail. "Come on, Sheriff, git that Miller feller out here or we're comin' in!" The sheriff raised his hand. "Listen, folks, I know how you feel, but Miller's my prisoner and I don't have to explain my job. Please go home!"

A burly man on a big dun horse waved a rope, shouting, "Let us have that killer, Sheriff, and save the county some expense. We'll git this over with right now. Let's rush that jail!" "Hold it right there, mister! Let me show you something," said the sheriff as he pulled a stag-handled Colt from its holster and with his left hand drew three silver dollars from a vest pocket. He tossed the coins in the air high over the crowd and with three quick shots centered the lead on the silver discs, which spun skyward at the ringing impact.

"Aw, Sheriff, what's that all about? We all know you can shoot, but you could only get three of us now and we'd take you and that jail," pointed out the man on the dun horse. "He's right, Sheriff, we've got a hundred guns out here. Give us that killer!" called a rawboned rancher holding a Winchester in the crook of his arm. Without rejoinder, the sheriff disappeared into the portals of the jail. He reappeared five minutes later, to confront the yammering mob.

He held three red cylindrical rods aloft in his left hand. "Now," he said, "you go home. Anybody raises a rope or a gun and I'm going to throw one of these dynamite sticks at his head and touch it off with a bullet!"

The mob slowly dispersed. A newspaperman from one of the Eastern dailies was admitted later in the day to the sheriff's office. "Sheriff, what in the world were you doing with dynamite in the jailhouse?" he asked.

"Dynamite, bunk! I went down the cellar and cut up a broom handle. What took me so long was I had trouble finding a saw."

THE SHERIFF

THE RAINMAKER

Every puff of hot wind raises more little dust devils which swirl and twist between the sage clumps and add to the ramps of dried-out topsoil heaped to the windward of every obstruction. Small clouds pass high overhead but never pause. The parched farmlands seem to writhe in the shimmering heat waves.

Down in the deserts the Indians have a dance to induce the rain-gods to come and bless their corn and squash, but up here on the arid plains the anguished settlers have worn their rain-prayers thin. There is but one more alternative—make up a purse and write for the rainmaker.

He comes, with his rockets and small cannon, his kites and explosives. A skeptical crowd of his clients gather on a knoll with an Oh-Lord-we'll-try-anything resignation.

Unlike his counterpart, the Indian medicine man, he chants no incantations nor does he move into a sedate dance. He sends up a kite which bears aloft a slow-fused bomb—a bone-shaking explosion! Then the cannon is loaded and primed—another jarring blast! Then a long pause while he sets up a line of rockets and fires them one by one. But no change comes over the molten sky.

The grangers assume more hopeless attitudes as the rainmaker sets his biggest rocket carefully for its highest trajectory. He touches it off with a four-foot match and it wobbles erratically heavenward. At the zenith of its flight it hangs for an instant, then explodes in one tremendous salvo.

The rainmaker goes to his wagon, pulls the tarpaulin over the bows and sits down on the tailboard under the canvas and re-lights his dead stogie. The sky in the west blackens as though someone poured ink on the horizon, then darkness rapidly covers the whole arc of the heavens. A flash and a deep rumble come out of nowhere and soon sparks of lightning are snapping groundward a few miles off. Then drops of water as big as dollars are splashing on upturned faces, but nobody ducks for cover. No, indeed—the settlers are doing a wild joyful dance that the Hopis could never hope to imitate.

THE FEDERAL JUDGE

HERE was no cud-chewing, feet-on-the-desk backcountry justice. Dusty he might be—from a thirty-mile buggy ride—but it did not cloud the sharp, truth-seeking eyes nor soften the set of his beartrap jaw.

Free from debt to local politicians, his decisions made law on the frontier a real and respected concern. He countenanced no drunken lawyers in his court and all six-shooters were checked with the deputy marshal outside.

Sometimes his courtroom was the back of a store, the counter serving as a judicial bench. Even a schoolroom took on an aura of the law's majesty when court was in session. The hanging lamps of a barroom illuminated a jury ranged along a wall, and the scales of justice cast deep shadows on the paintings of Bacchus and "Venus on the Half Shell."

Certainty of punishment was more of a deterrent to outlawry and crime than bushranging posses and gun-handy deputies, so that by the turn of the century the West had become more or less law-abiding and peaceful.

THE
BORAX TEAMSTER

Twenty-mule freight teams were not unusual in the early 1880's, but the Death Valley borax outfits were something quite out of the ordinary. The teams, actually consisting of two wheel horses and eighteen mules, hitched by a chain to a pair of wagons and a thousand-gallon tank trailer, stretched down the desert road for more than 150 feet.

The cargo was colemanite, which, until the discovery of kernite in 1926, was the most important ore of borax. The massive ore wagon and trailer hauled 45,000 pounds of ore over the 164-mile trail between Furnace Creek in Death Valley to the town of Mojave on the edge of the desert.

The teamster, with the help of his swamper, piloted the tremendous load over precipitous trails and across desert areas where the heat was often in excess of 140 degrees and the elevation at times was far below sea level. Great skill and experience were needed to drive over this kind of terrain. Also needed was a definite understanding between the teamster and his animals. Often, as the outfit was negotiating a sharp curve in a mountain road, more than half of the mules would be out of sight of the driver from where he sat on the near side-wheel horse working the jerkline with one hand and the brake line with the other. The swamper sat on the trailer wagon and controlled its brake as well as that of the following water tank wagon.

On the return trip the wagons were loaded with hay and grain for the mules and this was apportioned out for some ten stations along the route to be consumed on the way back when the wagons were again hauling a pay load.

WITH the grading of roads and scheduled stagecoach services to supplement the railroad came the tourists—to add to the natural hardships of the frontier. Most sight-seers rode the trains and stages, some jogged around on horseback, others pedaled high-wheel bicycles, and a few rode in their private carriages.

One of the latter—a good-looking, heavy but well constructed lady in duster and veiled hat—was seeing the West with her husband. They had viewed Yosemite's wonders and the phenomena of Coulter's Hell (Yellowstone Park), and now the travelers were driving northward over the red desert toward the spectacular chasm of the Grand Canyon.

Along the road, on the edge of the Navajo reservation, squatted a low adobe trading post. The trader, a booted leg hooked over the porch rail, was in earnest conversation with a handsome Indian. The Navajo, dressed in cotton trousers, soft boots, and a velveteen shirt cinched with a silver concha belt, was impassively listening as he leaned against a pillar. The trader was saying "But, Manuelito, I'd like to talk about that loan—" when the travelers' cabriolet turned into the yard.

The coachman stopped the carriage near the hitchrail and before he could put the wicker skirt guard over the rear wheel, the lady tourist had alighted. She went directly over to the Navajo and pointed to his silver belt. "How, Chief, wantum buy belt. How much?" she said. The Navajo shook his head negatively. She reached into her reticule and withdrew a purse which she oscillated under his fine aquiline nose. "How much wampum, Chief?" "No sell. This old family jewelry. When I get broke I hock belt with trader, get back later with wool-clip money." The tourist fluttered a fan of yellow-backed currency. Her husband, still seated in the carriage, wore a pain-

THE TOURIST

fully distressed expression. She added more gold-backed blades to the fan. "Come on, Chief. Heap big money now. Sell?"

The Indian looked mournfully at the fattened pack of bills and said, "Nuh." The tourist assumed a crafty look and her elegant fat fingers dived into the purse and emerged with a pair of gold double eagles. "How now, Chief, you sell?" "Sell, now," said the Navajo as he unclasped the belt, then handed it to her in exchange for all the legal tender.

As soon as the dust from the departed carriage cleared from the trading post yard the Indian reached up under the shirt and pulled down another concha belt, identical to the one now bound north in the cabriolet, and with a little smile crinkling in his black eyes, cinched it over the velveteen shirt. The trader said, "As I was saying, Manuelito, I want you to make me a loan to tide me over."

THE AUTHOR

Lorence F. Bjorklund has illustrated numerous books, both adult and juvenile titles, and many of them have had to do with the West which he knows so well. Born in Minnesota, he grew up in St. Paul within sight of the mighty Mississippi. While still in high school, he and a friend traveled the river's length in a sixteen-foot skiff they built themselves. The journey from St. Paul to New Orleans, 1,826 miles, was made in two months and eight days and was the beginning of a wanderlust that exists to this day.

After apprenticeship to a mural painter, work in sculpture, and lessons in drawing from his father, Mr. Bjorklund won a scholarship to Pratt Institute in Brooklyn. While attending art school there, he earned a living drawing Western illustrations for the then popular Western magazines.

Today, Lorence Bjorklund and his wife live in Croton Falls, New York. Summers are spent in South Thomaston, Maine, on Penobscot Bay.

Leisure-time hobbies include building models, making replicas of firearms of the Middle Ages, rebuilding precision metal-working tools, lapidary work, and wood carving. But, as always, drawing is Lorence Bjorklund's first love.